2-21-95

Melodee,

I am very pleased and honored that you would want a copy of the book!

Good Luck ī your practice!

God Bless you!

Dr. L Jackson

Days Gone By

M. L. Faulkner, D.O.

VANTAGE PRESS
New York

Illustrated by Ken Landgraf

FIRST EDITION

All rights reserved, including the right of
reproduction in whole or in part in any form.

Copyright © 1994 by M. L. Faulkner, D.O.

Published by Vantage Press, Inc.
516 West 34th Street, New York, New York 10001

Manufactured in the United States of America
ISBN: 0-533-10855-1

Library of Congress Catalog Card No.: 93-94154

0 9 8 7 6 5 4 3 2 1

To my wife, Tamara,
and children, Taylor, Ali, and Gentry;
each of them is a tremendous gift from God

Contents

The Taming of the Tongue	1
Saturday Nights at the Frights	3
A Moon over Paradise	8
An Oreo Surprise	15
You Get a Line, Tie It to a Pole, and Pull Me out of This Sewage Hole	18
Close Encounters of the Pathetic Kind	22
The Texas Two-Step	28
The Two That Got Away	34
The Dating Game	40
The Death of an Angel	46
A Night on the Town	52
A Day on the Farm	62
Days Gone By	68

Days Gone By

The Taming of the Tongue

The Bible indicates that it is not easy to tame the tongue. Through the years I have struggled with this, and I have witnessed many others doing the same. If a man's mouth indeed reveals what is in his heart, then hearts appear to be found lacking many desirable qualities. These thoughts and others, combined with the speaking in unknown tongues, have been the inspiration of many a Sunday sermon. However, when this topic arises I am sometimes reminded of an untamed tongue of another kind.

During college I made some extra money as a meat packer, and the old adage "you are what you eat" was observed by me on more than one occasion. When you looked in people's grocery carts you could just about place a bet on whether they were going to be extra lean or hog lard.

One day when I was checking expiration dates in the meat case, a muffled, lispy voice asked, "Tdoo youue haave amy bthef toongue?" Now when I looked up, my field of view was fully captured by the largest human tongue I had beheld up to this time. This poor soul evidently had some sort of nerve paralysis that had affected the muscle, leaving it somewhat uncontrollable and uninhibited. So there she was and there "it" was, just hanging around. Now I was at a loss for words as I just stood there staring at this large appendage, and again the lady repeated herself: "Tdoo youue haave amy btheef toongue?" Now several responses came to mind, none of which were polite or appropriate, but I bit my lip, restraining the humor that I found in this situation, and went to the freezer to search for a nice, large tongue that would be a suitable mate for the one already owned by this dear lady.

As I began to think once again about people taking on the appearance of what they heavily consume, uncontrollable laughter ensued. After regaining my composure, I returned to the customer and awarded her with a fine specimen of tongue. She was very, very grateful and responded with, "Dat's a beauutiful toongue," and I said, "Yes, ma'am, it sure is." Now I don't mean to be cruel and I know that the good Lord loves this woman just as much as he does me, or anyone else for that matter, and just so I don't make any of you angry about poking a little bit of fun at my dear friend the tongue lady, let me be fair about this. I've looked at myself in the mirror many, many times, and I'm quite confident that at some point during my childhood I consumed one too many chicken legs.

Saturday Nights at the Frights

When I was growing up during the years of junior high and high school, one of the big things around our house was scaring one another. I'm really not sure how this started, but I do know that I was always amused any time I watched a movie or television show in which people being scared either half to death or out of their wits was the main theme. It seemed to me there was nothing quite funnier than scaring my brother, my mother, or, best yet, my dad, simply half out of his or her mind. Of course it never was all that great when the time for paybacks came, and so I must admit it was a lot more fun dishing it out than receiving it.

One had to be really careful when scaring my mother. Mother was famous for throwing anything that she had either in her hands or near her at the head of whoever the offending person was. I made the mistake one day of scaring my mother when she was ironing and nearly caught that big piece of metal right between my teeth. She always let out a war whoop, just as she let whatever the object was go; therefore, you felt like you were being tomahawked by some Comanche Indian. Because of this I centered most of my focus on my father and my brother, who were much easier targets and certainly much less dangerous.

My brother was especially fun. He was very easy to

scare, because he would sit up late at night watching these Saturday night "Creature Features." Every Saturday night Larry would have a bunch of grub and soft drinks prepared in anticipation of Saturday night Creature Features. These were black-and-white horror flicks whose simple messages were camouflaged amid werewolves, vampires, and warlocks. Now the rest of us would already be in bed, but not Larry. He definitely belonged to the Creature Feature Horror Club. Well, late one night when I knew that it was about time for the last horror flick to be over, I decided to have a little Creature Feature of my own. I crawled under his bed, taking with me the vacuum cleaner hose.

I must have been under this bed for close to thirty minutes before my brother finally arrived. It took him awhile to get settled in, and I waited patiently under his bed, not moving a muscle. After about ten or fifteen more minutes I felt that he was about as ready as he was ever going to be. With one end of the vacuum cleaner hose attached to my mouth and the other hanging just outside of the bedspread, I began to let out a drone that I thought was very similar to what he had just heard over the last three hours downstairs. As I began to call him by name, moaning and groaning and breathing heavily, which of course was echoed tenfold because of the sound waves traveling through this small-diameter tube, there was no response from my brother. I continued this verbal assault on Larry for about five minutes, and having never gotten a reply, I assumed he was already fast asleep.

As I began to crawl out from under the bed I heard my

brother make his first sounds since I had started my groans and howls. It was hard to make out what Larry was actually saying, but it was soon evident that he was trying very desperately to speak. The fact of the matter was he was so frightened he was paralyzed. He couldn't move and he couldn't speak. He was simply trying to move enough air through his vocal cords to make some sort of sound. I felt pretty bad because I knew now that I had scared my brother half to death and the poor guy was lying there almost comatose. But never knowing when to quit, I reached up with my arm and grabbed my brother by his shoulder. He didn't flinch, move, or respond. Once again I heard him attempting to speak, and this time I could tell he was making an effort to call out my name. Now it was very hard for me not to break out in maniacal laughter at this point. In fact, after a couple of minutes of my poor brother lying there in this quadriplegic state, I did break down. When he realized who it was, he wanted to kill me, but he just didn't have the strength to get up out of bed. Depending on how you look at it, this was either the best or the worst time I frightened my brother. This experience practically aged him right out of his teenage years into adulthood. Afterward I did sort of feel bad about the whole thing, but evidently I hadn't felt bad enough or I wouldn't have done it. Anyway, he got me back a couple of weeks later when I crawled into bed and felt something cold lying next to me. When I turned on the light and rolled back the sheets, I saw Larry had placed the most real-looking rubber snake that I have ever seen in my bed. That was the night I became more familiar with the term *levitation*.

What about my ol' dad? Well, this story wouldn't be complete without letting you know what I did to him. Dad loved to watch TV in the evenings after a hard day's work, and if he didn't have a bowl of popcorn in front of him, he usually had a bag of potato chips. He was downstairs watching television, and I knew he'd be back up pretty soon and go to the pantry and reach for that favorite bag of chips. Therefore, I crawled up into the pantry after taking my shoes off and planted my bare feet on either side of that bag of potato chips. I was up in the pantry for probably fifteen minutes before Dad finally made his way upstairs. He stopped at the kitchen sink to get himself a drink; then he rounded the corner and opened the pantry doors. As I was looking down at my father, he seemed to be totally mesmerized by the cans of stew and beans and creamed corn and spinach. He was moving things around, kind of shuffling, gazing to see what he might open, without ever noticing me peering down at him from up in the pantry. Then he reached for that bag of chips, and at that point I could see my father's facial expression change. As he tried to refocus his eyes to convince his mind that he was actually seeing a bare foot on each side of this bag of chips, his mouth flung open. I'll never forget the horrid expression across his face, and I'll also never forget his hand coming up and reaching and grasping for his chest. He didn't look up at me at first; rather, what he did do was just fall completely back in the middle of the dining room floor. I never expected that reaction, but as he was lying there looking up at me and realizing who it was, I broke down with hysterical laughter. Dad was so weak with fright all he could do was look up at me and say, "Son, please don't ever do that to me again." I never did do that to him again, because I now began to realize that I was crossing over the line and taking this scaring game just a little bit too far.

Well, you know what they say: what goes around comes around, and I now have three children of my own. As it turns out, my son has an incredibly sick sense of humor. Now can you imagine that, and where, pray tell, did he get it? All I can say is chromosomes and genes sometimes just don't leave any doubt as to who your offspring are. My son is only nine years old, and he has scared me out of my wits on a number of occasions. Early one morning when I was taking a shower, long before I thought anyone else was up, I drew back the shower curtain to reach for my towel and grabbed a handful of body instead. At that moment retribution was made for my father. Now I'm looking ahead to the next seven or eight years that I'm going to have to deal with my son. I know that he has more in store for me, and I'm sure that as the years go by he will perfect his craft, just as I did. I know that his grandpa and Uncle Larry are very proud of him.

A Moon over Paradise

When I was a young man I had my dreams, as most young people do. Of course time has a way of humbling prideful imaginations, creating realistic acceptance of tarnished goals and failed finishes. Nevertheless, I don't give way easily, and determined to see the land that had impressed me so on the silver screen when I was a teenager, I instructed my wife, Tammi, to visit the travel agent and arrange passage to Tahiti. This tropical paradise had been on my mind since I was first exposed to it, by way of Marlon Brando in the movie *Mutiny on the Bounty*. Obviously, unlike Marlon, I would not be so captivated that I would marry the Tahitian beauty who had costarred in the movie. This was very understandable, since I was already married and no one had ever asked me to star in a movie, to begin with. Neither would I be able to purchase my own island in this heaven-on-earth sanctuary, like Brando was able to do. Even so, some twenty years after my introduction, I found myself on a jet bound to Tahiti.

I'm not much of an international traveler, and the flight to Tahiti was the first time that I had ever been over that great expanse known as the big blue. This was a little unsettling, but I knew that it was nothing compared to the adventures of Mr. Christian and Captain Bligh. So I settled back in my comfortable seat, which was almost wide enough, and reclined to that incredible ten degrees past perpendicular that is supposed to allow comfort and sleep! Some fourteen air hours from Kansas City and five time zones earlier, Tammi and I landed in Eden with youthful excitement despite paralyzed necks and the beginnings of bowel irregularity. We arrived just before the onset of a tropical storm, causing our connecting flight to Mooréa to be canceled. Six hours later we huddled together in a floating bathtub and bounced to Tahiti's sister island. I was not to be outdone, however, and had consumed massive quantities of Dramamine. The nausea did not come, but there was sort of a comical stupor from the medication, which in part was probably responsible for my sleeping the first fourteen hours after staggering into our bungalow.

The weather remained poor for the first few days, and the wind was strong enough to create certain doubts about the construction of the thatch huts. Tammi spent hours sweeping the roof off the floor. Even so, it gave us time to get acquainted with other American travelers who had shared this vision and dream of paradise. The initial slowdown was also probably the best way of preparing us for what was about to occur. You see, the people of Tahiti live longer in fifty years than Americans do in eighty. The pace we are accustomed to just isn't acceptable there, and you are literally forced to come to this screeching halt, whether you want to or not. I and so many others found ourselves ready to purchase spear guns, not for fishing, but to threaten the islanders with. After a couple of days, however, we removed our watches and slowed down. Suddenly, when the fight was

over, time stood still and relaxation began. Never in my life had I seen such beauty as these islands of Tahiti. The brilliant turquoise water, separated by mountains of emerald green, was truly a gift from God.

As we pondered this beauty and began to wonder if it could somehow give us a glimpse of heaven, reality sounded. Amidst the beauty stood the ruins of temples where virgins had been sacrificed to the pagan gods. Therefore, heaven had not been and still was not Tahiti, and there had existed brutal savagery among the garden of tropical green. Even so, the sailors of old had found the natives friendly compared to the cannibals elsewhere.

Outside the resorts, poverty was as clear as the native water. Those of us sheltered inside the lush confines could only appreciate this by mingling in the villages, and we did.

After satisfying our curiosity on land, the time came to brave the water. This I actually was not looking forward to. I knew there was no way that we could come all this distance and not experience the water, with all its coral and other life. Unfortunately, I had watched a program on TV before our departure concerning the sharks of Polynesia. So as I placed my mask and snorkel on, I prayed the Lord would spare me from becoming the special of the day for some overgrown meat grinder. Convinced that most of the big boys were out past the reef and remembering that days of pouring bloody chum were spent sometimes in search of the great white, and that there was no chum anywhere around me, I dove in. This was truly one of the greatest moments in my life. The quiet peace and surrounding marine life gave one the sense of truly being separated from the world above. This was my first time ever to snorkel, and I was thankful that our newly made friends were around to keep me from drowning after a few attempts at swallowing the sea. At one point I extended over a reef that dropped off into very deep water. The blue changed from bright to deep and rich. While I realized the greatness of the expanse that was before me, I turned and fled to the shore panic-stricken. For out of this deep surely would come the jaws of death, and I was making every attempt to walk on water. After reaching the shore, I got a grip on myself and returned, this time avoiding the deeper area.

The water was filled with fish. They were everywhere and of every color. All of them seemed to be congregating in one central area, and as I swam among them I noticed a long pipe lying on the ocean floor. The fish seemed so interested in this pipe, and for the life of me I just didn't get it. Surfacing and swallowing water, I asked my friend Henry if he knew what the fish were so excited about. He looked at me with a sort of sick surprise and informed me that we were over a sewage waste pipe. Ripping off my mask and snorkel, I started spitting, hoping to remove some of this excrement that I envisioned inside me. It was at this point that truthful realities began to set in. And although Tahiti was pretty, we were indeed still on earth. As I was drying myself off on shore, I was reminded that the beautiful fish feeding on sewage were not so unlike many physically beautiful people who are so full of worldly excrement on the inside.

Tammi and I made plans for the evening and found

ourselves dining on shellfish at the Blue Lagoon restaurant. Now before we had left on this trip I thought we would eat nothing but seafood the entire time. Seafood has always been a favorite of mine and this I was so looking forward to, but after the Blue Lagoon I searched high and low for any beef available. The day following our evening meal experience, I succumbed to shellfish revenge. For almost two days I stayed close to the bungalow with the most severe abdominal cramps I have ever had. Finally, when the diarrhea came to give relief, I was so bloated from the preceding constipation that I reminded myself of one of the blowfish I had found humorous before. And while all this was going on I was painfully reminded that time was running out in Tahiti. Tammi and I wanted to go shark feeding and to the barbecue on the *motu*, or outer island, and to the Lagoonarium. Despite my being very ill, I knew that it was now or never, so we hit the boat and left for the outer island tour. I made it to the shark-feeding excursion, and for me this was no small feat. There is something about feeling deathly ill that causes one not to care much about anything else. The sharks were not half as dangerous as the people we went with. As I was underwater filming the sharks feeding, one of the ladies next to me hanging on the rope nearly drowned me as she used me for a support in order to propel herself back toward the boat due to her fear. After the shark feeding was over we returned to our boat and traveled to the outer *motu*, and there the abdominal cramps returned. Stretching out under a palm tree, I was hoping I wouldn't have to relieve myself out there with nowhere to go. Finally, it was unbearable! In the absence of modern toilet facilities, I had to find relief out there among the coconuts, and getting back among the vegetation in an attempt to remove myself from sight, I left a little bit of myself on Tahiti. As if this wasn't humiliating enough, I was suddenly swarmed with some hybrid of gnat and mosquito that caused me to head for the water, bare bottom and all! As I squatted in the water, removing the evidence of the Blue Lagoon shellfish surprise, I felt like crying. However, I found the humor in all of this, because I know that I gave a whole new meaning to the phrase *a moon over paradise.*

A night later, Tammi and I were eating on the beach, toasting farewell to Tahiti with our new friends Henry and Rhonda. There were candles, traditional dances and music, the sound of drums, and the smile of my face as I looked upon the beautiful moon hanging over paradise. It was much more attractive than mine, I might add.

An Oreo Surprise

During the time that I was in the military service, I made many friends. Looking back, I cannot recall any more precious to me than my black buddies Kevin and Durell. The memories of them bring smiles to my face and a warmth to my heart. Each of us spent quite a bit of time together, sharing laughter and our opinions and beliefs about life. Since we were able to attend church together on base, it followed that we had many conversations about our individual religious convictions. It was this background that led the three of us to a tent revival on a warm summer San Antonio evening.

We discovered that it was a good thing we went early, because the revival ended up having standing room only. At first everything seemed "normal," and I say that realizing that "normal" is becoming harder and harder to define these days, or so they tell us. Truth has not changed through the ages of time, but people's twisted perceptions and weak convictions have helped to create incredible amounts of confusion. Anyway, as the program began, we found the message strong and convincing. The three of us were totally impressed. As the night grew on, however, it seemed the preaching began to take on different tones. Voices grew louder and the music became deafening. Emotions ran high, carrying with them the risk of poor judgment. Requests for money became numerous. The offering plate, the can, the apron, the bucket, and anything else that would hold money were passed, and people gave more than they seemed able to bear, according to outward appearances. Soon prayer requests poured forth and people began to line up, one by one, for the preacher, now self-proclaimed prophet, was going to provide the laying on of hands for healing. Now at this point let me interject that I certainly have no intentions here of making fun of or denying the power of God and the Holy Spirit. I say this because I am a Christian, believing in Jesus as the Son of God, and I have a healthy respect and fear for God the Father. Even so, the Bible proclaims that "by their fruits ye shall know them," and something about the fruit involved in this program seemed rotten. The service became louder, with yelling and clapping of hands replacing the calm and quiet time that had preceded. The level of "healing" had increased, until people were now being literally slugged into a "pit" that evidently had been prepared for this purpose. The pit was filled with straw, and we had had no idea that it was there before the service began. To our surprise, people would fall into the hole and seem to have seizures right there in front of us. They were actually foaming at the mouth, and I reconsidered what was really meant by the biblical Scripture of "tossing to and fro." As each so-called healing took place, things seemed to be getting more and more out of hand. As people lined up to be slugged into the rabid state leading to the pit "boogie," I suddenly was brought back to reality by the sensation of Durell's and Kevin's bodies pressing harder and harder against mine. Turning to look at their faces, I now realized our initial surprise and shock had been replaced with fear! Kevin's and Durell's eyes were now as big as silver dollars, and their faces had that sort of frantic look that usually precedes hysterical screaming, if you know what I mean. As both of my buddies pushed harder against my body, I realized that together we must have looked like an Oreo cookie, and at that point I could sympathize with the cream filling!

As the people lathered and foamed in front of us, suddenly Kevin came to his feet. As he was looking for an exit, Durell murmured, "If this is from God, then I'm the boogeyman." I agreed that the spirits present were not coming from up above, and we three were all in one accord. Sharing everything as we needed, our legs worked together and the then-created Oreo cookie with six legs fled from the revival, not one of us looking back!

Over the years I have lost track of Kevin. I still know where Durell is, and he loves the Lord now more than ever! I have found there are extreme differences between religion and Christianity.

Without question, this life is short at best, and only through contact with our creator do we find answers to the mystery of life. However, in the struggle to separate truth from fiction I am reminded of three young men, getting more so-called truth than they could handle, every time I pass down the cookie aisle at the grocery store.

You Get a Line, Tie It to a Pole, and Pull Me out of This Sewage Hole

Well, I was about fifteen years of age when I sought my first job. Oh, I was really excited about it. The opportunity to go out away from Mom and Dad and make my own money seemed almost unimaginable at the time. So out I went into the real world, filling out applications and having job interviews and planning for all the things that I might be able to buy with this income that I'd never had before. And so it was I was hired in a restaurant in Highland, Indiana, taking the prestigious position of a dishwasher.

Well, everybody has to start somewhere, and I was proud of this job. Minimum wage could purchase a fair amount during that time period, and I managed to get in about thirty hours of work a week while attending my sophomore year of high school. There were other duties involved in this job besides washing dishes. Tables had to be cleaned, along with the kitchen and the freezer. Supplies had to be stocked, etc., etc. Occasionally someone would become sick at the restaurant while eating, and of course, the busboys and dishwashers were always called upon with mop and bucket to take care of food that was still recognizable as roast beef, spaghetti, mashed potatoes, etc., howbeit, somewhat changed, and certainly not of pleasant aroma. With this first job I started building my savings account, dreaming of summer nights, a girlfriend, and my own automobile.

At the end of each evening when the restaurant was closing, part of the duties was to, of course, remove any trash and grease barrels from the restaurant and place it all in the dumpsters outside. Now restaurants do have a lot of trash and garbage, and it doesn't take long before these big waste cans inside the kitchen become pretty heavy. So my small one-hundred-pound frame would drag these trash cans out at the end of every business day, groaning with all the might I could muster up.

One evening there was something different about the path that I normally traveled with these waste cans toward their destination. I did not notice it, but evidently someone had been to the restaurant earlier that day and cleaned out the septic tank located in the parking lot. The thing that he had failed to do was place the manhole cover back in its original position. And so, while dragging out the trash, without any warning, my small body suddenly disappeared from the parking lot. To this day I cannot imagine how I managed to fall directly into this sewage system through such a small manhole-type opening. It was as if I fell off into the Grand Canyon, for I just slipped in so easily. So there I was swimming in liquid dung and feces and whatever else imaginable in this septic system, fearing that I would drown in the waste before I could pull myself out. As I climbed out of the so-called sewer, I was literally covered from head to toe with materials that I had previously always been able to flush away.

Regaining my composure, because I was somewhat shocked, I walked back into the restaurant. Those of my buddies inside who didn't immediately see me could certainly smell me, and soon I had everyone's attention. You would have thought someone had yelled, "Fire!" because everyone was evacuating my vicinity in quick order. There was gagging and pinching of nostrils and quick movement, and this was the first time in my life that I had ever felt like I was suffering from a plague.

As I thought more about this occurrence, it dawned on me that I could have actually drowned in this sewage system. No one was offering to help, and now I was becoming angry. I couldn't believe that whoever the idiot was who was involved in cleaning out this septic tank had left the cover off, and before I had really fully comprehended what I was doing, I found myself walking through the restaurant on the way to the manager's office. By that time I had evidently gotten used to the stench that had been permeating my nostrils, for it didn't seem to be bothering me as much as it was everyone else. But as I walked through the restaurant, among tables and people attempting to enjoy their dinner, I certainly brought about quite a commotion. Of course the manager gasped in horror when she saw me, and after I told her what had happened she quickly escorted me out of the vicinity of the poor people who had been trying to have a nice evening meal away from their home kitchen. As she reassured me of her sincere apologies, I climbed into my car to travel home.

I'll never forget the look on my father's face when he opened the door to find me standing there, dripping with toilet tissue and turds, smelling of stale urine, and very humiliated. As my father washed me off with a garden hose, I started laughing. I couldn't help but think of all the times he probably had felt like whipping me for acting like a little poop, but this was one time when I really was!

My next job was sacking groceries at one of the local supermarkets. I would sack groceries all day long, mop the floors, put the stock away, and find anything else that I could do to avoid taking out the trash.

Close Encounters of the Pathetic Kind

The emergency room is a hard place to earn a living. Most people have little understanding of the sacrifice that it takes to become a physician, and of all the different specialties in medicine, I'm convinced that ER work is one of the hardest. Of course one realizes that it is impossible for someone to understand someone else when he hasn't worn the other person's shoes. For example, I cannot understand the man who's defended his country in war, for I have not done this. So in return I would not expect someone to have a great deal of compassion or understanding for doctors or nurses when he or she has not undergone the rigors of that training. There was a time when doctors seemed to hold an elevated place in society, and maybe that place was too elevated, but it's certainly anything but that now. Physicians seem to be in the public spotlight, often thought of as sons and daughters of wealthy people who have been given everything in life, earning little, if anything, on their own. Most of the time this is not true. While doctors do earn a comfortable living, the majority of them are not excessively wealthy. Most of my colleagues work very hard and extend many financial courtesies to those who are less fortunate. Sure, as in any field, there are those who are arrogant, selfish, and dishonest; however, the majority care about people very much and will do their best to help, even when not paid for their services.

All this aside, I liken the work of a doctor in the ER to that of a soldier in a combat zone. There are sometimes no clear winners in this game, only givers and takers.

The system is clearly one of abuse, for very little that comes into the ER is truly an emergency, making it very bad on the few people who truly need emergent help. Coughs that have gone on for a month, back pain for a year, belly pain since last Christmas, are just a few of the routine ER Saturday night specials. Then there are the abuse offenders and victims. The weekend can barely go by without a drunk or two who have crashed their truck into some unsuspecting soul, leaving it to you to break the news to the family that their son or daughter is dead, while the cause of the accident is in the other room waiting for your attention, which you are legally obliged to give. Of course, this story wouldn't be complete without the mention of physical abuse. Sometimes a wife is beaten so badly, with multiple contusions and even possibly fractures, that she is barely recognizable. No charges are filed, and the offender impatiently awaits in the lobby for this abused person to return to him. Medical personnel involved can only hope that next time it wouldn't happen on their shift. In the inner cities I have seen syphilis, gonorrhea, and men dressed like women. You may be able to imagine my dilemma in trying to remove an antiperspirant can from a willing rectum that gave new meaning to "I just want to be Sure." Then I recall the gentleman who was sent to surgery with a phone cord hanging out of his male genitalia. When asked why he did this, he stated that he was only trying to "reach out and touch someone."

It would be tactless and in poor taste to comment any further on these and other instances. I don't mention these accounts to glorify them as much as to show my disgust. A person could cry, but in an attempt to remain sane at 2:00 A.M. personnel in the ER sometimes become hardened and numb. Needless to say, it is because of experiences such as these that I quit inner-city ER work, and my prayers are with those who still make their living providing this service. With these thoughts in mind I recall one other evening in Youngstown, Ohio, that ultimately and convincingly revealed to me that I was no longer fit for inner-city ER work.

It was late in the evening on a weekend when a gentleman came into an already-busy ER demanding treatment for abdominal pain. It wasn't long before he had disrupted what peace remained in this so-called people zoo. My attention became focused on him, in hopes that I could get him out of the ER before his profanity upset the sick kids and mothers. Soon it became apparent that the patient was not acutely ill but instead wanted narcotics. When I refused to give him any, he became even more abusive. Finally, he began to taunt me and follow me around the ER. I instructed the nurses to call security and have him removed. Subsequently I left and went to the cafeteria to get some coffee, hoping that by the time I got back he would be gone.

To my dismay, when I returned he was not gone, and matters had gotten even worse. Security was not responding to the call for help, and so I requested that the local police be called. Before police help arrived, this societal parasite was using profanity and calling me names hard to accept. While the nurses and other patients looked on, I realized that the fine line separating rational and irrational behavior for me was being crossed. During this period of time in my life, I was in training for boxing's Golden Gloves in Youngstown, Ohio, and as a result was tempted to have someone ring a bell so that the sparring could begin. My last attempts to remain calm and in control failed me, and I finally turned on what had been my patient, now turned abuser. I instructed him that in order to qualify for narcotic medication one must have sufficient injury and/or pain. Since he didn't currently qualify, it seemed only logical to help him get what he came for. Pinning him in the corner, I exploded with bottled wrath and frustration that left this pitiful soul begging for mercy. Instantly the nurses were on me, holding me back, and it was only this that saved me from striking this man with combinations that would have undoubtedly cost me my job, even though he deserved the punishment. The outcome was okay, since the patient stopped his verbal assault and cooperated with the Mr. Hyde that had emerged from this Dr. Jekyll.

Later in the cafeteria, trying to soothe my altered ego and nervous dementia, I realized that despite the unmerciful studies in med school that had created such emotional and physical strife, I was not prepared to be a physician. How could anyone prepare you, after sacrificing the best years of your life, for these kinds of sicknesses? Years later, as I reflect on these close encounters of the pathetic kind, I wonder how

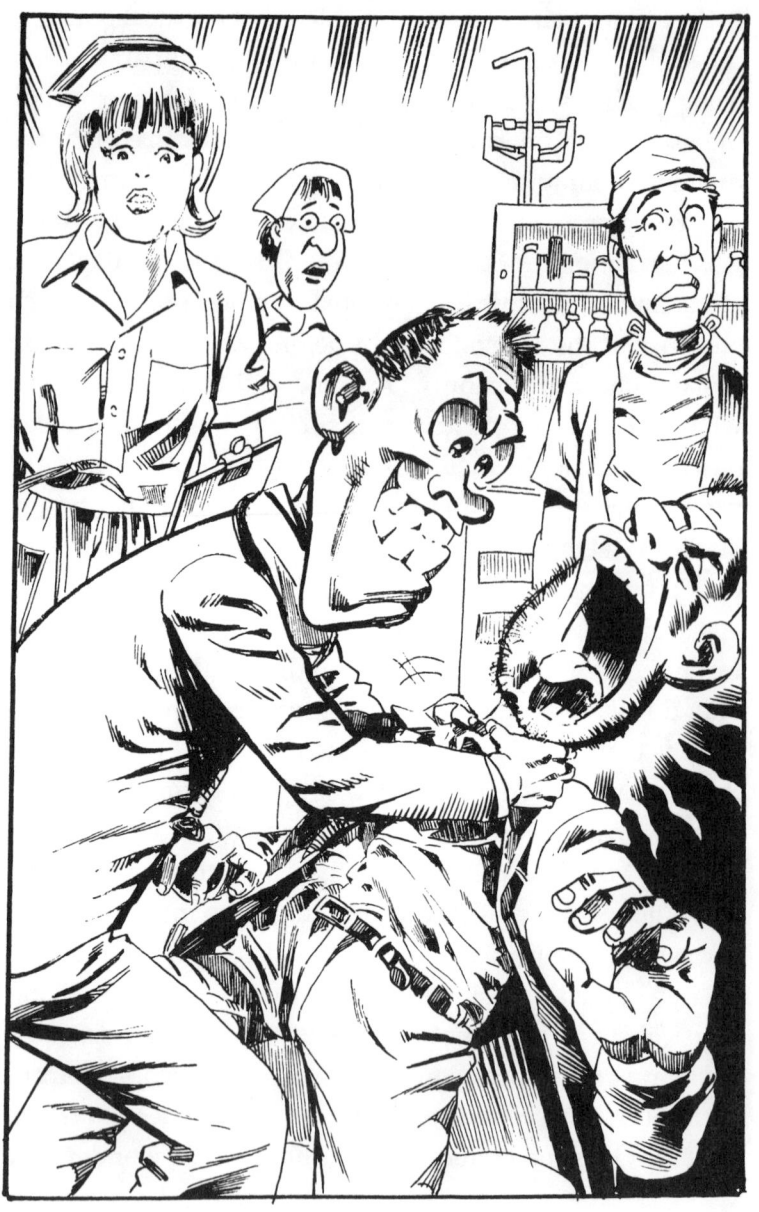

much of a pay cut I should take so society will feel good about me and my profession again. Since our heroes are now HIV-positive athletes who brag about their sexual encounters like notches on a gun and seemingly mentally disturbed rock stars wearing propellers on their brassieres, I suppose the answer is clear. Society is truly sick, and doctors can prescribe no medicinal cure for these diseases even if it were to be free.

The Texas Two-Step

I have always wanted to go deep-sea fishing ever since I read the book *The Old Man and the Sea.* The vivid descriptions by Hemingway in this book created a vision in my mind of blues and greens that were almost beyond his descriptive abilities and my imagination. The majestic fish soaring high out of the deep in an effort to free itself, allowing only a brief glimpse of its power and strength, would truly be something to behold. Therefore, when Tammi and I were in Texas for my six weeks of active duty with Uncle Sam, we ventured down to the coast around Corpus Christi in search of an oceangoing vessel that would take us to the waters of the sailfish.

Upon arrival, to our dismay, reality began to set in. First of all, things have changed since Ernest Hemingway's tale of the old man's sea. Replacing the old man with his little outrigger were some old men with some very expensive motorized cabin cruisers. The amount of money that was required to rent one of these vessels for a mere four-hour period, with no guarantee of coming into contact with the marlin, was quite a bit more than Tammi and I were able to find in our jeans. Therefore, not wishing to be denied, we began to look for the economy package. We found ourselves standing in line with about fifty other people who had not found enough money in their pants either. Boarding a boat that looked somewhat like a bathtub and forming a circle around the boat, each of us was issued a glamorized cane pole. We looked forward to catching something, but it was doubtful it would be a marlin or sailfish. As we left shore and heard people talking about the storm that had just subsided, I began to question in my mind if we had made the right choice. Now I knew that as a child I had many, many problems on the merry-go-round. I also realized that a carnival ride in my teens had left me on a sofa for two and a half days believing that it was time for me to meet my maker. I was not exaggerating then by telling Tammi that myself and motion just didn't seem to get along, especially when it was that type of motion that causes one to go round and round.

The farther we got from shore, the rougher the waters became. I don't know how far we had gotten out from shore when I began to realize that the sun appeared to be rising and falling in the sky, as if morning and evening were almost happening simultaneously. Let's put it this way: if the storm in fact was over, I would not have wanted to have been there when it was occurring. These waves certainly seemed anywhere from six to eight feet tall to me, and that would be a conservative estimate. The boat was rocking, and I do mean rocking, when I finally looked over at my wife and said, "You know, I'm not going to make this." Tammi bravely and wittingly told me that this was all in my head and to just try to get a grip on the situation. She then said that she would leave and come right back with some soda crackers for me that would settle my stomach.

Now while Tammi was gone I began to try to think about

very nice and pleasant things. I made every possible attempt to put what was happening out of my mind. But before she returned, I realized that whatever she had thought was in my mind was now in the pit of my stomach. Like a fool, I was standing on the upper deck, and so I began to bob and weave my way to the ladder, that I might climb down to the first deck of the boat. I met Tammi about halfway down the ladder. As I turned and saw that she had several soda crackers in her hand, I reached and grabbed for them, ripping them away from her and stuffing them in my mouth, somehow believing that they would give me an instantaneous cure. Before we left the dock I had consumed a large amount of shrimp cocktail. As the crackers went down, the shrimp cocktail came up, and the projectile vomiting that ensued was so powerful that my wife, ducking out of the way, allowed the shellfish–soda cracker combination to capture the attention of many of the passengers standing by. As Tammi escorted me over to the side of the boat, I proceeded to puke myself into what I can only describe as a vegetative state. I was convinced that my stomach as well as half of my intestines were hanging out of my mouth, being dragged along the side of the boat. Even so we proceeded unrelentingly toward a so-called fishing spot, among these hideous waves. As I continued to retch until there, of course, was nothing left inside, I recalled looking up at Tammi and stating to her that I wouldn't care if the biggest shark that had ever been seen would come up and bite my head off just to put me out of my misery. Tammi told me that I was as green as my shirt, and it was widely spread all over the boat that there was a poor young man dying.

Now I was not the only one. There were several others who had started the puking process. We had obviously been ripped off. Our money had been taken, and the captain of this boat was bound and determined that we would reach the fishing spot and then all beg to come home; thereby he would have plenty of reason to keep the funds. Something was for sure: he was not going to stop. He was on a conquest. Even though there were others who were sick, apparently I had won the prize. The ladies who were working in the restaurant of this bathtub came and got me, took me inside, and laid me down on a cot in this sort of cabin/restaurant/bar. They advised me to suck on a dill pickle, of which I bit off, swallowed some, and quickly regurgitated it. Finally there was nothing left to do but lie there and suffer, with Tammi wiping my face off with a damp cloth. About three hours later we made it back to shore with several sick people and, of course, no fish. Yes, that's right. No one caught a thing. I practically crawled off the boat and was totally unable to walk without assistance. And as I was groping along I, to my embarrassment, saw one of the gentlemen that I had vomited on earlier. You see, the wind was so strong that it had captured some of the regurgitations coming out of me and on a couple of occasions had thrown it on someone else's shirt or face. I don't know if you can imagine the humility and shame that I felt in this, but at the time I was so sick I almost didn't care.

Tammi and I stayed on the dock for a long time, as I was

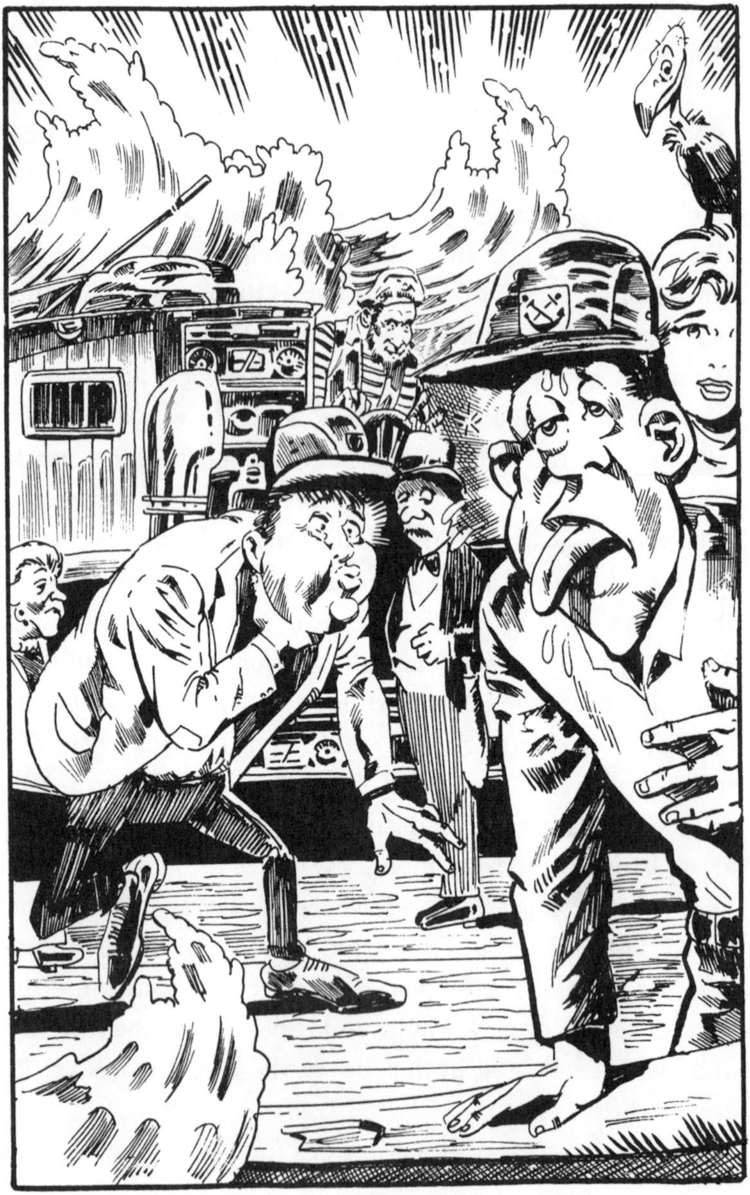

just trying to get my head to stop spinning long enough to tolerate the drive home. I was unable to eat shrimp cocktail for several years. Never since then have I attempted to go deep-sea fishing. Recently I again read the book *The Old Man and the Sea*. Eventually I may get up the courage to try again, but only after consuming massive amounts of medication known to be effective for motion sickness. Also, you'd better believe that I'll have appropriate funds in my jeans so that I can secure a different boat. As well, I'll be seeking out some weather information to make sure there have been no recent storms.

So I still dream of emerald green, majestic blues, and sailfish jumping out of the water, giving everyone a glimpse of their beauty. But along with my imagination fed by the descriptive and talented abilities of Ernest Hemingway captured on the pages of a book as he wrote about an old man off the coast of Cuba will be my memories of the time my stomach and I danced the Texas two-step on a revolving dance floor known as the Gulf of Mexico.

The Two That Got Away

Mike and John were two brothers from New York who obviously missed their calling. These brothers appeared to be perfect candidates for the Mafia; nevertheless, here they were in northeast Missouri packing books and notes to medical school rather than guns to confession. Mike and I were in the same class and John two years behind. For some reason, known only to God, Mike and I developed a friendship during this time of torment that has stood firm through the years. We certainly did not have a tremendous amount in common, for I was a Southern-born Protestant hillbilly who thought that doing evil was chewing gum in church. On the other hand, Mike's Italian Catholic background would seem to place us on opposite ends of the totem pole. Despite these overwhelming differences, there was a similarity that seemed to make all the difference. Neither of us was tall enough to make five-foot-six even with boots on. This curse of near dwarfism had caused both of us to suffer from Napoléon complexes accompanied by delusions of grandeur, enabling us to exchange war stories together about our various persecutions. Thus a great bond was formed.

Mike and John desired and desperately needed to be acculturated for their plunge into Midwest living. They reasoned that the perfect person to take on this massive project of reprogramming was, of course, myself. However, the one thing they did not count on was my incredibly sick sense of humor, which I believe I inherited from my grandpa. Grandpa was a mischievous sort, and I recall when I was a child his talking my brother into tickling a calf's balls and then watching him laugh hysterically when the calf kicked my brother halfway across the barn.

Now Mike and John had heard a lot of the guys in class sharing tales about eight-pound largemouth bass caught in farm ponds, and they felt compelled to venture forth. On a summer afternoon they asked me to take them farm-pond fishing, and I took on the challenge. We gathered up fishing tackle and headed out for the wild country.

During the ride to the farmer's pond I could hardly contain my sinister thoughts as I realized that in my hands were two people who, for a mere moment in time, were more naive than myself. I didn't know how, but I felt the need to have some fun with these New York mobsters, just to make my grandpa proud by carrying on the family tradition.

When we arrived at the gate, John asked me where the pond was and I told him it was quite a distance out in the pasture by the trees. Mike then wanted to know if we would be driving out to the pond, and I told him that I didn't think the farmer would appreciate that, so we must take a little hike. It was then I recognized an opening.

Mike and John seemed troubled by something, and finally it was John who revealed what was bothering them by asking me, "What about all those cows?"

Now here it was, hanging out like Mother's clothes on

the line. I knew that in order for me to have fun with this my answer would have to be smooth, perfect, and very sweet, without any hints or traces of mischief. It is moments like these that everyone with a sick sense of humor yearns for. I knew that I couldn't smile or laugh or give them any indication that I might be up to something. Therefore, I kept my reply very short and direct. I simply said, "Don't worry about the cows; they won't bother us." So we crossed the gate and headed for that great beyond and I contained my hysterical thoughts and suppressed laughter, for I knew that revealing these emotions would mean that the moment of terror for Mike and John would never come. As I began to imagine in my mind what was probably about to happen, I thought that at any moment horns would come thundering out of my head and my hysterical groans would be the kind that would top the "best hits" list in the local psychiatric hospital. Despite the battle going on within, I restrained myself.

Sure enough, as we crossed the distance nearly fifty head of cattle in the field began to fall in behind us, and the distance between myself and the two brothers seemed to become less after each step.

Mike and John were now eyeing the cattle very closely, and it was John who uttered the first words. "Why are the cows following us?" he asked.

At this point I wanted to offer something cheap, like telling him, "Because they are going to eat us, John," but I knew that would finish it, so once again I restrained myself and replied, "Don't pay any attention to them," repeating that they weren't going to bother us. After this reply I intentionally walked a little bit faster, knowing that the cattle would keep the pace, looking for the food that just wasn't there.

Mike was notably getting a little more nervous now and seemed to be focused on a Hereford off to his left. Once again I had to contain my laughter, because it seemed that Mike had almost singled one of the cows out in case this became a fight. At this point if this could have been a movie I would have asked for angelic singing in the background of "When I've Gone the Last Mile of the Way," for it would have been perfect. The cattle were getting closer and closer, and I knew that I would have to act very soon.

John, now with just a hint of anger in his voice, said, "Look, Lynn, what is this deal with these cows?"

I now knew that it was time. Mike and John were just too impatient to be put off any longer. So I asked, "John, are the cows closest to us the red ones?"

He replied quickly and emphatically, "What difference does that make?"

During this exchange of conversation I was walking just a little bit faster and faster, with the cows also picking up their pace in response. Mike and John were all but on my back now, and I felt that the vine was ripe. I then stated, "You know, the red ones can get just a little bit aggressive." And, with just a little bit of hesitation in my voice, I turned and faced the cattle very quickly, and I screamed, "Good Lord have mercy on us, they're attacking us!" I threw down the fishing tackle, wheeled around, and started running as fast as I could. The cows did not disappoint me, as they sounded

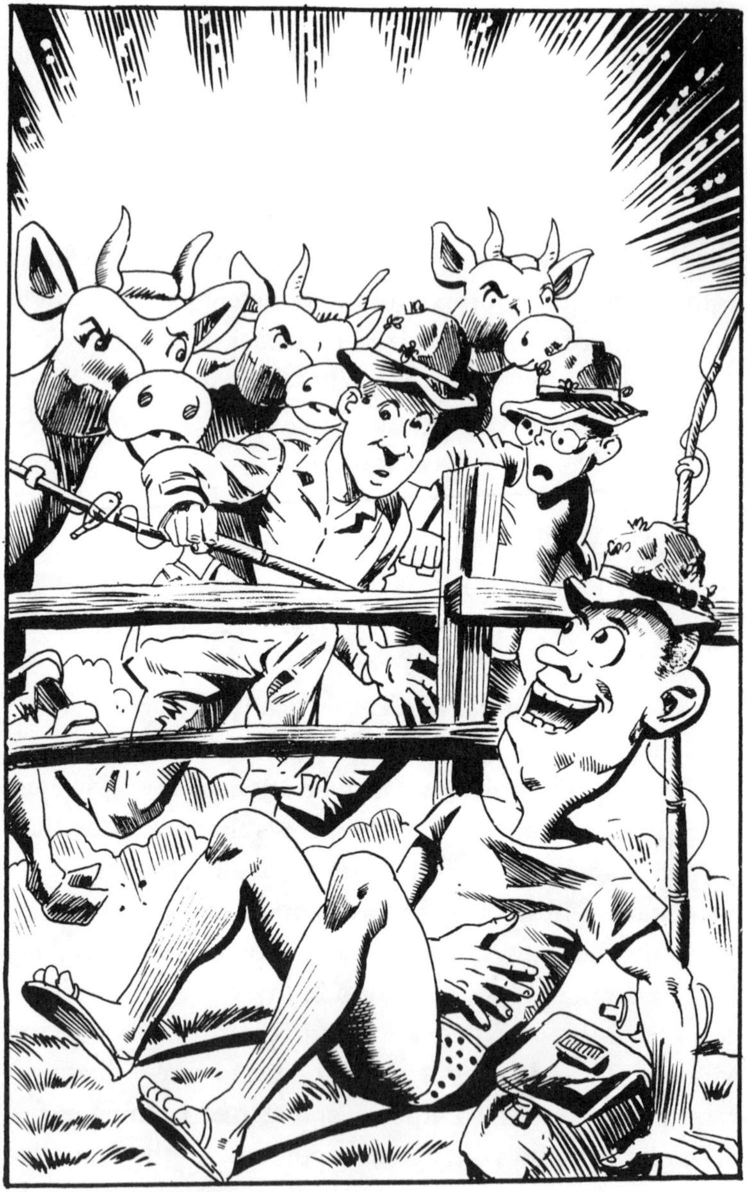

like a herd of buffalo thundering in hot pursuit. Now when Mike and John went by me they reminded me of the cheetah that I saw as a child on "Wild Kingdom." Their acceleration was very similar, and the expression on their faces reaffirmed my belief in life after death!

Mike and John cleared the barbed-wire fence around the pond with the ease of deer, and once I was over the fence I collapsed with hysterical laughter that caused me intercostal tenderness for days.

I have been on many fishing trips since this one, but I have never been able to top the tale of the two that got away!

The Dating Game

At twenty-seven, I decided to marry. Since the age of sixteen I had dated, and during this eleven-year period I had my share of frustration with the dating game. Frankly, when comparing notes with others, I might say that I had more than my fair share. How I ended up with some of these people defies imagination. To tell all of these accounts would require hundreds of pages. I have been horrified, electrified, mystified, surprised, and downright frightened half to death. Some of these events were not funny at the time, especially for someone as naive as I was during the younger years. Like the time I was waiting for my date at her house when her mother decided to share her library with me. Her collection of books on witchcraft and werewolves was a little unsettling, and later that night when I was watching TV in the basement, the electrical appliances starting turning on and off without any visible assistance. This caused me to reconsider my attraction to this female, and during a brief intermission from the current ruling authorities I disappeared in a fashion that would have made Houdini proud! Or perhaps the time I was stood up on a date and went to the girl's place of employment the next day to find out what happened. When I tapped her on the shoulder in the bowling alley, she turned and screamed, "Don't hit me!" Even though I had no idea what she was talking about, she repeated this so loudly that in shock I ran from the bowling alley with horrified embarrassment, which probably made me look guilty as sin. Anyway, I could go on and on! I will spare you all the gory details of many of these dating experiences if you'll just allow me to tell you about one more!

I was sacking groceries at Strack and Van Tills in Highland, Indiana, when one of my buddies said he would like to introduce me to his sister. Well, what can you say to an offer like that? Later I realized that there was more than one answer to this request, and through the years the answer "no" became an easier response. She was a pretty gal. In fact, she was very pretty, and immediately I thought I was in love. At the age of nineteen you can imagine how little time and consideration went into this "concrete" decision that I was in love. Incredible as it may seem, about thirty seconds after I met this girl I felt that I knew that she was the one. Yes, that's right! We were married with kids, and everything was heaven on earth, fireworks every night, bells forevermore, Samson and Delilah, Romeo and Juliet, Sonny and Cher?! . . . Well, you know what I mean. All of this and more, just minutes into the relationship! Wow! Isn't true love great?

After our date, I was at her house sitting on the couch when I suddenly got a funny feeling, that feeling you get when someone is watching you. I still recall how strange it felt. It was a scary experience. I started looking around the room, and upon gazing at the front door I began to think that I could almost see someone looking at me. When the lights are on on the inside and it's dark on the outside it's sort of hard to figure out what you can see and what you can't. Anyway, I was so star-struck by the beauty I was with that I figured hallucinations were a possibility. So I laughed it off. Then a little while later, as I was unable to shake off the feeling that someone was watching me, my eyes returned to the door. This time I decided to ask for a second opinion. When I asked Nancy to look at the door and tell me if she saw something, she screamed and fled to the back of the house as if she had seen a ghost! During her flight, I thought I heard her mumble, "Darrell." Then I heard footsteps running around the house and suddenly there was a pounding on the back door. Well, one thing was for sure: I had seen someone! Meanwhile, Nancy was coming back down the hall with her mother in tow. They both seemed very frightened. The fact was that they were so white that they blended into the walls. Nancy's mother gasped that it indeed was Darrell. They both grabbed me and led me down the hall, then they opened a closet and shoved me into it. For a while I stayed there among the shoes and coats, as if this seemed a rational thing to do. I must admit that there was some sense of security in that dark place. I listened to them talk about the situation. They even argued about what to do. There was talk of murder if he found me. There was mention of calling the police. Suddenly I realized that I was at the house of a girl I barely knew, with a maniac outside trying to beat the door down. Better yet, I was in a closet in the house of a girl I barely knew with her and her mother talking of my imminent death. As my mind began to return, causing me to realize that this was not a nightmare, it struck me that the monster of the porch certainly knew that I was in the house, and being trapped in a closet probably would not save my life. Therefore, I emerged form the dark abyss and, with the confidence of a Barney Fife, sort of convulsed down the hall.

As I struggled free from the two women who were again trying to put me into a closet, I boldly stated that I refused to be held a prisoner after only one date, and I requested parole. They did inform me that I would certainly be executed if I tried to escape. At this point my anger began to surface. I felt that it was time for me to find out who Darrell really was. As it turned out, he was none other than Nancy's old flame, with whom she had broken up only one week earlier. Since that time he had threatened suicide and driven his car into a ditch. Now Darrell was tearing the back door off the hinges to try to destroy the evil within who, he undoubtedly reasoned, was me. I asked the two sick comedians to call the police, but they responded that they did not want to get Darrell in trouble. I found this very humorous for about thirty seconds (as you recall, about the time it took for me to fall in love), and then I picked up the phone to call my dad. After a couple of rings I realized that I was nineteen years old and calling my father to come and get me from this girl's house seemed like a rather immature thing to do. Looking back, it probably wasn't such a bad idea. However, with the ego of a nineteen-year-old I hung up the phone, figuring this was my fight and my problem.

Well, it was time for this party to end. I turned and while the two beauty queens fled to the sacred closet I opened the door.

Darrell was at least six-foot-one and clearly somewhat disturbed. Looking down upon me, he grimaced and stated, "I'm going to kill you."

Now, even though I must admit that I was frightened, I was also sort of disappointed. After all, Darrell's entry had been rather creative. With a little thought he could have been more imaginative with what he had to say. If, indeed, I were about to die, it would at least be nice being killed by someone a little more articulate, I thought. At five-foot-five and 130 pounds, I've not intimidated many people. However, even though small physically, to my credit I was a wrestling champion and weight lifter and, frankly, I resented being so small and never really liked being pushed around by big people. Some might say that I was sort of defensive about this. I decided to let Darrell have a piece of my mind, and I remember hoping that this would be the only piece of me that he would get! I explained to Darrell that I had no idea about him and Nancy, but I told him that I wasn't prepared to die just for being there, and if I had to pick something up and belt him over the head with it I would. What happened next left me standing there in total disbelief; Darrell collapsed on the couch and began to cry. The two maidens quickly went to his rescue. Nancy's mother gave Darrell a couple of tranquillizers to take, and meanwhile Nancy sponged his face and head with a cold cloth. While I stood there staring in total amazement I realized that I was free to go and poor Darrell had what he wanted—my place on the couch. I really don't remember how long it was that I stood there, but eventually

Nancy turned toward me and stated, "You can go now; I think you've done enough!"

On the way home I began to realize certain truths about love and the dating game. First of all, it takes more than thirty seconds to know someone very well! And also, when one decides to keep company with a beauty, check for beasts! They may not be friendly.

The Death of an Angel

College graduation was only four months away. Most of college had been hard, due to employment combined with a premed curriculum. If things could only have been that simple perhaps I wouldn't look back on these times with such anguish. Complicating things even further, however, was the divorce of my parents, as well as my mother's great emotional and mental difficulties. The trials and tribulations that led to the divorce, which I would rather not remember, added to my mother's struggle for survival, caused me to feel that the weight of the world was indeed on my shoulders. As I fought to continue my education, which had been so insisted on by my mother, I tried to understand what it was that was troubling her. My ability to do this was very limited, and Mom seemed to be dying daily, with less and less to live for. Eventually she was attempting suicide, so my father, my brother, and I all reunited with Mother, in an attempt to reclaim the family we once knew and the woman who meant so much to all of us. We sought professional help, but it failed. As the three of us men fought over what to do about Mom's depression, the sickness in our family reached new heights. Since the fighting and pressure between us seemed endless, I decided to go to a friend's house for the weekend. My mother suddenly seemed to feel better, and the evening before I left she cooked dinner for the family. We sat together and talked about the old days, giving a glimpse of hope to us all. She kissed me in the driveway and informed me that she would always love me, reassuring me that I had been a very good son.

I left my father, brother, and mom that night with confused feelings about life in general. Guilt overcame me that evening, and so the next day I phoned home. Mom answered and everything seemed okay. Dad and Larry were at work, and I knew that she was alone. Her spirits seemed better, though, and she asked if I had decided to come home. It seemed to me that another night away from home might ease the tension between Dad and Larry and me, so I told her that I might return the next day. As I hung up, everything seemed stable.

I decided to stop at the grocery store and pick up a few items for the dinner that my friend and I had planned for that evening. As I pushed the cart around, I began to think of my family and why it was being destroyed. We had been happy and seemed to enjoy each other's company the majority of the time. Our family had attended church, but this became less frequent as my brother and I reached high school. Looking at my watch, I was reminded that my dad would soon be home from work. About that time I began to feel very troubled. From somewhere deep within I knew that something was wrong. Maybe the thought of my mother and dad being there alone troubled me, or perhaps I was now realizing that she had been alone for too long. No matter what the reasons were, I began to panic and frantically started looking for a phone. There was no answer at home, and now I was totally convinced that Mom was in trouble. This moment in time became so emotionally charged that I felt my very soul was being ripped from my body. It seemed that while I stood there a part of me inside was literally dying and it was totally against my will. Quickly I phoned a neighbor and, to my horror, she explained that an ambulance had been to my house. As I ran from the store I realized that by the time I got to the house the ambulance surely would have left for the hospital. Therefore, I drove directly to the hospital, and once through the emergency doors I looked around, and standing there with his eyes glued to me was my dad, still in his work clothes, covered in the black soot from the steel mill that I had seen on him so many times. I froze, and from across the room my dad and I sank into empty darkness that gave new meaning to "the bottomless pit." As the dam broke inside me, the tears poured forth testifying to my grief, emptiness, and despair. My friend, companion, soulmate, and lifegiver was gone. What was left of me sat there next to my father waiting for nothing but permission to see the remaining shell of a being I once laughed and cried with. Dad never had to say anything, for I knew by the horrified, empty expression on his face that Mother was dead. Soon thereafter my brother arrived. So the three of us huddled together, much like an athletic team out of energy and time, accepting defeat. Dad elected not to go in and see Mom, but my brother and I felt that we had to touch her one last time. She was cold, blue, and swollen, and her spirit was unreachable. Her lips now did not receive mine with joy, neither were they tender or loving, but I pressed harder, determined to extract a memory to cling to. My brother cried and uttered some words that Mom had longed to hear from him for years, simply that he loved her. One more time I told her that she had been the best, only this time she couldn't hear me. We prayed for Mom with eyes that were now almost as edematous and swollen as hers and kissed her good-bye forever on this side of eternity. This woman who bore me, changed my diapers, took me to piano lessons, cheered in the bleachers for her boy wrestler, witnessed my baptism, and loved me more than herself was dead. In a moment of desperate agony, this flower had fallen by her own hand.

Now, two months before graduation from college, instead of planning parties with family and friends or choosing professional schools, I was preparing for a funeral I wanted no part of and selecting a coffin for my mother. As family and friends gathered for the tribute to this person who had been so torn and tattered that death was welcome enough for her to invite, many things came to my mind. Mom had only acted as if she were better so she would be left alone long enough to get the job done. Of course, I now knew she seriously intended to end her life. Now I remembered her requests one by one as they hauntingly returned to my consciousness. Respecting these wishes, I made sure she was buried in the dress she had hand-picked for this occasion about a month earlier with me in the privacy of her bedroom. Hymns were sung that at one time I had played on the piano for her to sing.

While sitting there drained with agony, I listened while

the minister referred to my mother as a fine diamond he had the pleasure of meeting. She was so beautiful and bubbly and had always been the life of the party. When my high school buddies came over, I never was clear as to whom they wanted to see more, me or her! So what had happened to destroy this woman? Apparently she discovered that her love for her husband had vanished. Her children, being grown, were not in need of her as before. She loved God, but religion had left her empty, searching for any visual evidence of true Christianity. Not believing that there was any moral solution for her unhappiness, she resolved that there was a home more suitable for her beyond the confines of this earth. Her love for everyone seemed to have run out, as it appeared that it was often more than she received in return. There she would find peace, joy and comfort returning to the giver of life, whose presence is undeniable despite so-called noble intellectuals' reasoning otherwise. It was here at her funeral that I began to call her insanity into reason and thereby attempt to gain strength and understanding. This understanding would be needed to comfort me in the coming months and years, in which I would struggle with overwhelming guilt for the hours I had left my mother alone by my own choice.

Relationships between my father, my brother, and I were strained for many years, and I am sure that it will always be somewhat difficult until the time comes for each of us to cross over Jordan. As we live, eat, marry, work, and finally die, how many people ever stop to count the cost? What meaning is there in this life of broken promises and dreams without the peace of a relationship with Almighty God? Here is where life begins and ends. This indeed is the only truth this side of eternity, and I discovered all of this through the death of an angel!

A Night on the Town

A few years ago, at thirty-two years of age, I paused for a moment after a long day of work at the hospital for some reflection. At the tender age of eighteen, becoming a doctor had seemed like a noble effort and it had impressed family and friends. However, the years that followed extracted a heavy toll. College, air force, med school, and now residency had accounted for them all. And although thankful, I felt cheated. It seemed that the fight for the prize is sometimes so tough that the prize itself becomes somewhat diminished in value. Realizing that my youth had been spent in search of career thrills and satisfaction, I felt a sense of eerie emptiness. The death around me seemed to be stealing my passion for life. I recalled the high school athletics that caused those adrenaline surges, now only provided in ampules for patients. Indeed, this career choice had left me tired, disappointed, and numb. The idea then came to me that defies logic to this day. Even so, it allowed me to feel that youthful surge of energy once more, while also serving to remind me that reflection isn't always healthy.

I presented my thirty-two-year-old body to a local boxing gymnasium and introduced myself to the trainer. He seemed puzzled but somewhat entertained by my sincere intentions. My persistence won out and the boxing gloves were strapped on my hands. I stepped into the ring without any experience and sparred the last year's Golden Gloves champion. Two minutes and a broken nose later I understood the meaning of pain! Since my high school athletic days, my only contact with conditioning had been occasional running and some semiserious weight lifting from time to time. This, of course, was irregular, secondary to the time-consuming academic demands. However, what strength I had managed to retain was probably responsible for saving my life during this brief introduction to the sport known as boxing. I indeed felt somewhat foolish at this point, lying in the corner, with my head up, attempting to stop the free flow of blood from my nostrils. My intellect told me that I needed to leave and forget about this temporary insanity that had overcome my ability to reason. The embarrassment was just too much, however! Isn't it amazing what we'll do for the sake of pride? Therefore, I returned the next day, swollen membranes and all, and began to hit the heavy bag.

For a week I returned to the gym, despite Tammi's pleading for me to help her raise the children before I was bludgeoned to death. Finally, the trainers realized that I was intent on carrying out this mission, and so they started showing me a few tricks of the trade. By the end of the week, my trainer told me that he was taking his boxers to fight in Erie, Pennsylvania. He asked if I would like to tag along, and I thought it might be fun to watch, so I agreed. Then came the real clincher. He wanted to know if I would like to fight on the card along with the others. Now I knew that doing all this for the first time at the age of thirty-two had left me with several disadvantages. Certainly my friends and colleagues believed that this was a crazy idea. Also, taking a fight after only a week of training couldn't be expected to give me that desperately needed edge! My recollection of high school wrestling days, the amount of work and training that was demanded by that particular sport at the tender age of seventeen, served to remind me that there must be an error in judgment on the part of this so-called trainer! His response to my initial decline to this offer was to remind me that if I was going to do this thing I might as well get started. He convinced me that I would survive this contest; if I really expected to compete in the Golden Gloves it was time for me to get the show on the road. Unbelievably, there was a touch of credibility to his argument, but there was the issue of conditioning that seemed to escape the thought process that was occurring at this time. Three three-minute rounds seemed like a long time to me, and I knew that the gloves had felt like concrete blocks during the fractured nose incident. Of course I had not healed from the injury yet either. He persuaded me, however, and the next Friday evening, after baby-sitting services were arranged, Tammi and I found ourselves in a van heading for what would be one of the most frightful experiences of our lives thus far!

It was not hard to detect which side of town the gym was on once we got there. The area was rough and dirty, and once inside I realized that I'd made a big mistake! The ring was already covered by stale cigarette smoke, and there were motorbikes everywhere. The show, as it turned out, was being sponsored by the Hell's Angels, of all people! Bearded and generally hairy men were everywhere with black leather jackets, chains, knives, and size 13 boots. One or two of these guys looked like something out of the World Wrestling Federation! The women were tattooed in certain strategic places and didn't appear to be the type that would be involved in cross-stitch or the PTA, if you know what I mean! My wife was now sure that I had indeed lost my mind, and at this point I was inclined to agree with her.

I left Tammi on a folding chair at ringside and went downstairs to a locker room to weigh in. Fighters were getting dressed and shadowboxing, apparently sizing each other up. Tension filled the room and conversation was very limited. My nerves were getting the best of me now. I realized that I was not ready for this. My imagination began to take over, and the fear of humiliation was draining any ounce of strength that I had left. While my hands were being taped I looked at the man who had talked me into this nightmare, and I managed to utter my disbelief that I was actually going through with this. He reassured me that I was going to survive, but in my mind the fight was already over, for I defeated myself.

At that moment I didn't feel like I could have whipped a sack of potatoes! My legs were numb and weak, and my heart was in need of cardioversion, for the fear now was just beneath that level required to make me fall on the floor and have a seizure! I would have done this, but I was sure that even if I had it wouldn't have helped me get out of this fight, since it was becoming increasingly apparent that this trainer was going to have me fight even if he had to drag me into the ring himself. Therefore, I began to size the trainer up, trying to determine if I thought I could whip him and escape from this slaughter that I was convinced was about to occur! I knew there were two problems with this type of thinking. Number one, I had no ride home, and number two, my arms felt like rubber bands. So we made our way up to the gym among the crowd and we positioned ourselves close to the ring. The number of people packed into this small gymnasium was unbelievable! This had really turned out to be quite a fight show, and at least it was some consolation in knowing there were going to be so many witnesses to my murder. Tammi was in tears by now. She came over to show me a copy of the program and also appeared to say good-bye! According to the program, my opponent was nicknamed "Caveman." About that time our eyes focused on one of the hairiest, scariest men that I've ever seen. He was throwing punches wildly in the air and had a look on his face that assured me that he was out to destroy the next person who crossed his path! I felt a tremor go through my body as I now realized that this was Caveman!

The fight was drawing near, and I needed to know one final thing before I climbed in between those ropes. Could it be possible that he, too, was a beginner and things would turn out all right? I found myself uncontrollably making my way toward him, and tapping him on the shoulder, I boldly asked who he was. It was Caveman all right. I so wish that I never asked him the next question. His response of having been in nearly forty fights, most of which were in the penitentiary, resulted in my testicles being sucked into my abdomen and my tongue becoming so swollen that I couldn't continue any further conversation. I tried to turn and go back to the area where I had left my trainer, but my left leg was frozen. I don't recall entering the ring, and suddenly I found myself standing there staring at this huge maniac, dressed in nothing but jeans and a leather vest. This six-foot-six giant was the ring announcer, and I couldn't understand a word he was saying. People were screaming and shouting, uttering the word, "Caveman," during the barbaric introduction from the cyclops in the center of the ring. Just then I realized my opponent was in my corner beating the turnbuckle pad. With this, I wheeled and turned to my trainer, who I was now convinced hated doctors and was in need of psychiatric help, to ask what this beating of the turnbuckle was all about! He replied, "He's just trying to psych you out." Well, since my hair felt like it was on fire and my legs were totally paralyzed, I had little doubt that his strategy had worked!

I heard the bell sound, barely. I now knew that punch after punch was hitting me. My face, my body, my arms, my belly, my legs, I even thought I could feel my toes getting hit. He was everywhere that I was running! There was nowhere to turn, and there was nowhere to hide. What a sight I must have been, with toothpicks for legs and rubber bands for arms. He was beating me senseless, and I could feel the warmth around my nose and on the canvas was a trail of blood that marked where I had attempted to flee the scene of the crime.

Suddenly a bell rang and I was being assisted to the corner. I felt a towel and water. A doctor was looking me over, and my so-called trainer was applying pressure to all the needed areas. When he asked me how I felt, I so badly wanted to vomit on him, but I couldn't spare the energy! I did hear what he had to say, however! He reminded me that I had survived. I had taken Caveman's best shots, and even though I offered nothing of my own, I had survived. He stated, "Now, how do you feel about it? Do you really want to be a fighter? Well then, this is the time to let it go."

When I got up I knew what he was trying to tell me and sensed that it was time to see if I had anything to give back. God above must have heard my cry from that ring, because at that point I could feel the fear in me begin to fade and my strength return. The bell sounded and Caveman came for me, but this time I met him in the center of the ring and threw my first punch. My fist found something, for I felt the shock wave that ran up my elbow and into my arm and finally into my neck. For a moment he was not there. The moment I threw the punch my eyes had been closed, and by the time that I opened them I saw my opponent staggering in front of me and then turn and limp over to the ropes. People were now jumping and screaming, and the noise was so deafening that I could not understand or hear anything that made any sense. I was in total shock and disbelief! I remember questioning in my mind if I had truly hurt him. He appeared to be moving again, but now it wasn't directly toward me.

I remained in this position for what seemed to be an eternity before it came to me that I should pursue him. When I cornered him, I called upon what was left of me and began

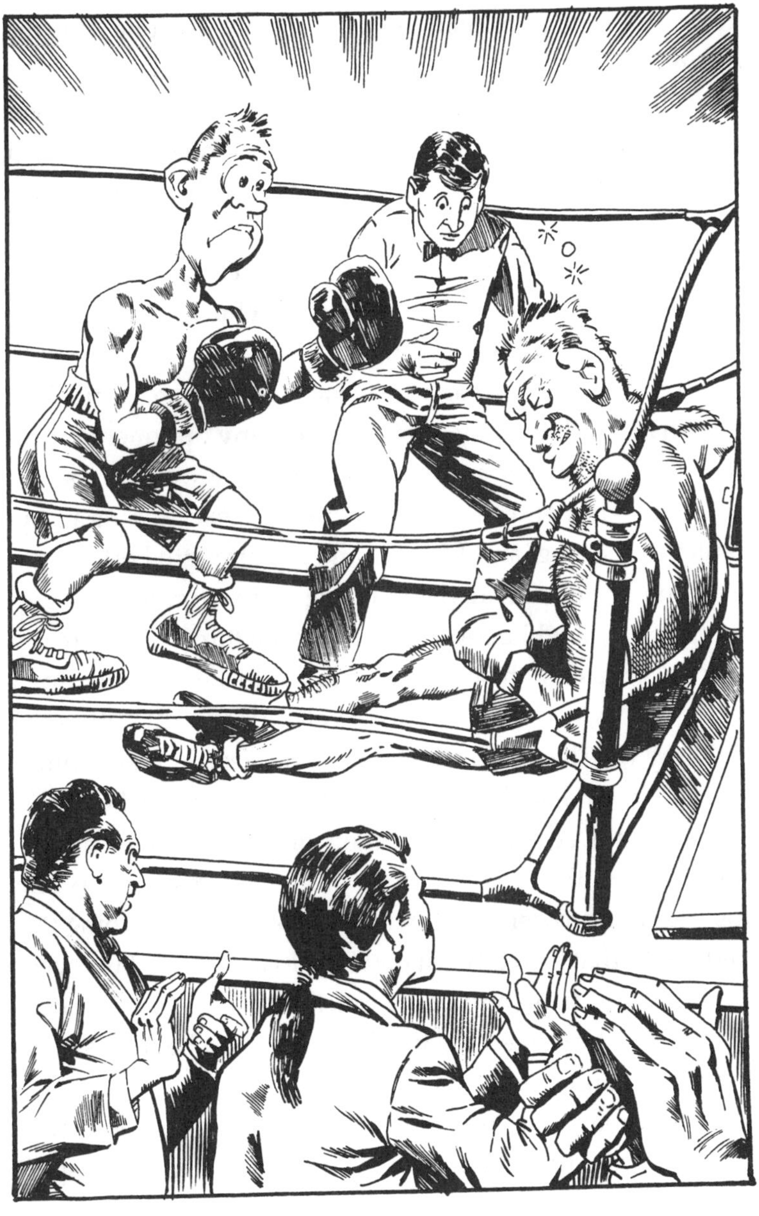

to do my best to exchange with him one for one. But the instinct to try to hurt or finish him just wasn't there.

The bell sounded and I returned under my own power and was told that I had won the round. The doctor visited me again and checked my nose; it was still bleeding steadily. But I was the one this time who assured him that I was fine, for it truly wasn't notably bothering me. The physician, now realizing that I was a doctor myself, just chuckled and stated, "Go for it. You can win this fight."

The bell sounded and I was now ready to respond. The right hand followed by a left hook left my opponent crumpled on the ropes for a moment, and he recovered, issuing another right hand to my nose. We were exchanging in the center of the ring, and I felt his and my strength both giving way. In my peripheral vision I caught the glimpse of something. It was a white towel that had been thrown in from my corner! I was astonished that this could be possible, for I knew the fight would soon be over. Apparently, before the fight my wife had made the trainer promise her that if things got out of hand or if I was getting beaten too badly he would stop the fight. Apparently the show of blood from my broken nose caused this gentleman to panic and resulted in him tossing in the towel. Afterward he apologized for doing this and stated that he really felt that I could have won. I was very upset, since I had endured so much of this memorable evening just to be denied the finish of what had begun as more than just a night out on the town!

A year later and with the help of two other trainers, who had a more educated approach to the aspects of the sport known as boxing, I became a Golden Gloves champion in Youngstown, Ohio. I entered the ring of combat only six times before I hung up the mitts in my short career. I had known the agony of defeat and the thrill of victory, as they say. The fear I indeed experienced that Friday evening never returned again in any of the other bouts I had. My concern now is growing old and not being able to tell my grandkids about Erie because of the failing memory. For as long as God gives me breath during my short stay on this planet, I will always remember Erie as the night Tammi and I returned to adolescence and all its insecurities, combined with youthful excitement.

Here's to you, Caveman, wherever you are.

A Day on the Farm

A few years back, I decided that I wanted to purchase some property in the country. I had heard a lot about the good life. Fresh air, peace, relaxation, no crime, raising your own beef, a place for the kids to run, and all the other great things that have given credence to "the good life." Shortly after the purchase, and after making certain the fences were in order, I embarked upon the purchase of cattle and any other critters that I thought would be necessary to qualify this modest six acres into my perfect little farm. Now I knew that I was not knowledgeable about the art of cattle buying; therefore, I was somewhat reluctant to go to the market, for fear that I would bring home some pathetic beast that would contaminate my little piece of heaven with sundry various diseases. I reasoned that some of the neighbors in this part of the country would be willing to part with a few head of these animals at a fair price.

Now Pete was a tall, slender fellow, and evidently he and his father made their living farming. They had several head of cattle and also several calves that were well on their way to "cowhood." I proposed to buy a few, and Pete seemed very happy to cooperate. Pete was rather unusual in his efforts with conversation, as he had seemed to develop this nervous habit of spitting. He talked very, very fast, and with this continual spitting it was really not easy to communicate with him! I found myself looking and watching in the apparent direction of his spitting to see if he actually could be producing enough saliva to sustain this brutal pace. After a while it seemed evident that there really wasn't much coming out of Pete's mouth other than words, but he never broke stride with his spitting. Anyway, I returned home expecting the delivery of two young calves within the week.

A few days later, Pete arrived with three young calves on his truck. After close inspection, I noticed the calves were a little smaller than the ones we had spoken about. I questioned him and he informed me, while spitting of course, that he had been to the market and purchased these calves for me. Well, this was a little disturbing, since this was of course not my original intent, nor my instructions for Pete. He assured me that these three were a great deal at about the same cost as two of his, and I reluctantly agreed to accept them.

A couple of days later I noted that one of these animals was acting just a little bit strange by comparison to the others. This one calf seemed to be standing off alone, away from the other two, and wasn't eating very well. This continued for a couple of days and I phoned Pete, but he assured me that there were just some initial adjustments the little critter had to make. So with Tammi's purchase of seven goats from another local farmer it seemed like we were well on our way to a little piece of heaven.

A couple of days later, after returning home from work, my wife and I noticed a few very large and unusual birds hovering over our place. Gazing from the window as we were bringing the garden hose through it to fill our water bed, I told my wife that I was pretty sure that these giant fowl were the same types I had seen in many of the old cowboy shows. Therefore, I meandered across the field to see what the party was about. Sure enough, here was my little calf lying under a tree looking like one of the helium balloons in Macy's Thanksgiving Day Parade! This was quite nauseating, and by now I was more than just a little bit upset!! I called Pete and invited him over for the barbecue of this pride Angus that he had so graciously delivered, but he declined.

After consultation with a local veterinarian, it was decided that the animal must be incinerated and I set out to move this calf to an appropriate place. I was quite confident that my four-wheel-drive truck could handle the job, and I attached the animal to my vehicle by cutting a hole through the ankle with a knife and running a chain through it.

I was pulling the animal up out of the field when suddenly the load lightened just a bit. After getting out to see what had happened, I noticed that the leg of the animal was coming up the ravine just fine, but the rest of the animal had decided to remain where it was. Now this was just about all I could take! Pulling the leg of this calf behind my truck was not my idea of a way to relax after a day's work. Returning to the scene of this severed blue-ribbon classic, I affixed the remains once again to the Ford. This time I made sure that my attachment was secure, but not without gagging due to the putrid stench that was permeating my nostrils.

Meanwhile, Tammi had arrived on the scene to tell me

that one of the goats was apparently choking on something and had collapsed in the other pasture.

Well, at this point I was overcome with a real need to laugh, figuring if I could find a little humor in this perhaps the spell would be broken, but the groan that came out of me was more like that of a hyena in heat! Running to see if I could save the animal, I contemplated the feasibility of performing the Heimlich maneuver on this full-grown Nubian goat. I certainly couldn't conceive CPR.

When I arrived the animal was in such distress and suffering that I became overwhelmed with compassion, and despite all my efforts to upright the panic-stricken animal and clear its airway, the animal was obviously strangulating to death right before my eyes. I went back to the house to retrieve my rifle to dispose of the creature, for I could no longer bear its suffering. Upon my return, the animal was standing but cyanotic and laboring for breath. I aimed and shot; however, nothing happened. When I realized that I had actually missed this animal with my 30/30 rifle, the panic set in!

I could now picture that the trajectory of this bullet had traveled down the hillside and killed one of the neighbors' children or something horrible such as that. I now would be considered a crazed maniac that had gone on some shooting rampage, killing everything in sight. I was ready to pass out at this point! My wife and kids were all crying, and we all had a new definition of the term *funny farm*. Trying to get a grip on myself, I walked back to the house, retrieved my pistol, came back to the animal, and this time left no room for error. We had given all the goats names, and now Barbara was out of her misery. The whole affair made me so sick, however, that the bathroom toilet and I became very intimate for a while.

A short time after, I was again in my truck, and this time with both a goat and a calf in tow. The calf and the goat were burned together, and I just knew that all our neighbors were now discussing what type of people had moved on top of the hill. As we were standing over the animal sacrifices, I'm sure that we appeared to be in some sort of weird cult. As the sun went down on my six acres that evening, I was reminded of a simple truth: "the good life" isn't something you purchase, and that greener pasture on the other side of the fence might be better left alone! That evening my wife and I sat on the sofa, attempting to calm ourselves, when suddenly we looked at one another in horror and got up and ran to the bedroom. At that time I discovered another excellent rule for living: do not become distracted while filling your water bed.

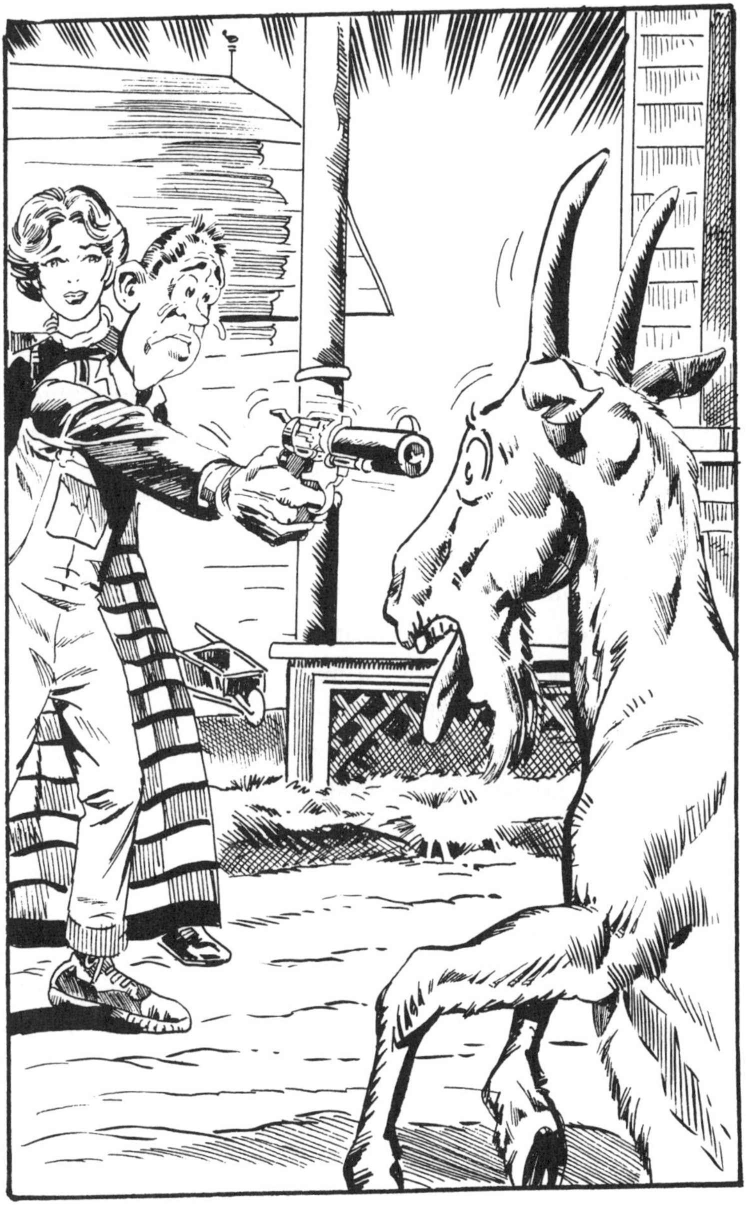

Days Gone By

This summer, God willing, I will attend my twenty-year high school reunion. Should I get to that day I will reach what most consider a milestone in life—that is, a reunion with boys and girls whom I grew up with. Sometimes age eighteen seems like such a long, long time ago, and yet at other times it is as if it were only yesterday. Now one would hope that these twenty years, post–high school, would account for something. I'm sure at the class reunion most of us will try to convince our former schoolmates of just that. We'll all compare notes, trade horror stories, and possibly even keep score as to which of us have done the best. I intend to make every effort not to play that game and just pray that in my own life there has been some growth, wisdom, and insight gained from the experiences that I have had over the years. For every detailed account that I've recalled in this book there are certainly several others that I will not take the time to write about. Even so, there are just a few more that I will mention briefly.

I can recall my first fight in the bathroom at school in seventh grade. It was there among the stalls and urinals that this ninety-pound weakling finally got tired of being picked on and decided that turning the other cheek wasn't always necessary and could potentially prove dangerous to one's health. How can I explain, especially being raised with Christian values, the pride I had after being declared the winner in this bathroom brawl? All I know is the bullies didn't bother me anymore after that experience.

Having always loved old cars, I couldn't wait to show all my college buddies the 1953 Dodge that I had purchased. So I took them along with a cousin and a brother to a lake outside of Chattanooga, Tennessee, on a beautiful summer afternoon. The Dodge was indeed a beautiful classic of its day, and it rode like a dream. However, on the return trip home the brakes went out as we were driving down an incline. While friends and relatives screamed, I struggled with the parking brake in order to keep us from going off the side of the mountain. Having barely survived that, the car's engine then promptly exploded, leaving us all stranded on the side of the road. A few days later, when I'd managed to have the ol' classic towed back to the car dealership, I became educated with regard to some used-car salesmen. The gentleman's response was to laugh maniacally when he gazed upon the vehicle then turn to me and state, "You know, son, this is how you learn your lessons in life; you never should have bought that old piece of junk." Since I couldn't afford to have the engine completely rebuilt, I walked away and left the old Dodge, and I haven't been really interested in vehicles over ten years of age since.

When I completed basic training in the U.S. Air Force, I was very pleased to be asked to be a scientific research assistant at Brooks Air Force Base in San Antonio, Texas. I imagined being involved in some very interesting research, and in time I was. However, my involvement was quite different than I had presumed. It wasn't long before I had been submersed underwater, taken to extremes in both hyperbaric and hypobaric chambers, and walked for miles on inclined treadmills donning fire-fighter equipment at chamber temperatures of 110 degrees Fahrenheit. As a part of the fire-fighter equipment study, both esophageal and rectal thermistors were placed to record my body core temperatures. So I learned that scientific experimental research involved two parties. May I say that I served my country well?

So as we struggle to stay young by watching what we eat, exercising daily, and keeping our appointments with plastic surgeons yearly, always reaching and straining for that achieved goal, desired result, career choice, or a suitable companion who will give us that peace and contentment that we so yearn for, we soon realize that this was a game we were born to lose. We appear to be always a day away from where we ought to be. What then is the truth that I have gathered twenty years past high school graduation? To me it is becoming more clearly apparent every day that King Solomon was correct. He stated that there was nothing new under the sun and man should enjoy the fruits of his labor during the short days of his life, for this is his lot, given to him from God. Happiness, then, is not something that we should seek and yet so seldom find, because it must come from within and surely is a state of mind. We know that we will take from this earth exactly what we came in with: nothing. I have a bumper sticker on my truck that states: "He who dies with the most toys wins nothing."

So we laugh, we cry, we fight, and we die. The world keeps on turning, and in all of it, where are the reasons for the why? My friends, the peace that passes all understanding does indeed come from the Word of God. By spending time in this Word and also on our knees we develop a life-style that is harmonious with our creator. Not having that relationship is to leave one void of any ability to give significance to life. The Good Book says the end will come within a twinkling of an eye. When the Lord returns this time it won't be as the meek shepherd boy, but a king. On Judgment Day we will be separated and placed into but one of two groups. The Bible classifies these as the sheep and the goats. After all the effort we make to be somebody, the college studies, the career aspirations, the fight for money, fortune, and fame, we are simply categorized based on what we did or didn't do with regard to a relationship with our Redeemer.

What, then, about the next twenty years? Undoubtedly there will be many more stories to tell. I will probably meet more good, decent, honest, Christian, law-abiding citizens. Unfortunately, I will also come across people who claim they believe in nothing but the pleasure that they can squeeze out of any one particular moment and could really care less if it happens to be at your or my expense. I'm sure there will be more laughter, joy, humiliation, defeat, and triumphs. Let me therefore reach out to all of you, my earthbound companions.

Since not another second of life can all your money buy, and you, too, will someday lie down to die, I sincerely hope and pray that you will take time to reflect and find meaning in your days that have already gone by.